ELIZABETHAN

I

JONATHAN LOVEJOY

Jonathan Lovejoy

ELIZABETHAN

The Complete Poems of Elizabeth Peele

Volume I

Jonathan Lovejoy

Cover: *The Pearl,* 1894
William Adolphe Bouguereau (1825-1905)

ISBN-10: 0692319166
ISBN-13: 978-0692319161

For every Elizabeth

Introduction

Carmen Angelina Coletti (Elizabeth Peele) was perhaps the greatest composer who ever lived. After her death, studies of her music revealed a body of work—almost exclusively instrumental—of such beauty and power as to defy description. Even so, her lifelong reclusiveness rendered them obsolete to the world, and these musical treasures may remain apart from public view forever.

Even those few who heard her original scores did so in quiet apprehension, that this beautiful widow—lost somewhere deep in North Carolina farming country—brought forth music as completely ingenious as any ever written before. The sounds of greatness flowing from this woman's piano, surely this is not meant to be! For what purpose can she truly serve as a neoclassical composer in a jaded modern world, except as a curiosity and eventually, a fountain of eternal exploitation?

But while music did serve as a profession for her since she was twelve—her only wage being a sound mind and spirit—there was still another expression, both private and unintentional, equally meant for her eyes only. Gathered posthumously, so few of these "assemblies" can be called unique or special, and likely cannot set her apart from any other lonely poet in the world. But still they live on, as a glimpse into the mind of a musical genius and abused woman of Faith. Written parallel to her music over the years—with no striving for greatness or immortality—these poetic trifles, ironically, may be the only compositions of hers the world will ever hear.

Jonathan Lovejoy

ELIZABETHAN

or

"The Assemblies"

Jonathan Lovejoy

Elizabethan

Such is the grandest music among us—

Poets...

Such are the wildest thoughts among us—

Composers...

The Book of Elizabeth

1st Assembly

Jonathan Lovejoy

1

Indian Summer
Thy glorious departure!
Colorful season of Death
Echo of nights in Winter

Cold rains descend
Through an Autumn mist of gray
Wet, weeping world
Frozen in regret

Days of mourning
Joyful summer's passing
Eternal grief and sorrow—
Gladness for nature's sleep

\

2

I saw Death far away from me
Power lifted the cold winds
When leaves of color drift and swirl
Its touch is removed from my soul

Heaven was revealed in the clouds
Striking fire in the hearts of men
Resurrection from the fear of Ages
Rest from dark and painful years

Haunted by these Mournful spirits
Only sadness, no curse of gray
Paradise for another time—
Another eternity

Elizabethan

3

O Dreadful Serpent!

Desireth my body and soul
No commission from above
Thy wicked hands are bound

Thy evil image
Puts laughter in my veins
Thou art powerless
With fruitless devastation

Fearful creature
Prince of Darkness
Condemned pawn of Fate—
Defeated enemy of mine

4

The angry blackbird
Calls me from the grave
No claim to my body
This evil minion of pitch

Thy dreadful calling
Is now music to my ears
No flesh for thy craving—
Nor blood for Hellish thirst

An empty coffin
No futures interred
An Almighty vow—
Cry of an angry blackbird

5

What fruitless endeavor!
Gripping my immortal spirit
A longing for the ages
My eternal desperation

Her beautiful name
Sings God's promise to me
The Desire of mine heart
Fire in my immortal soul

Love's Humility
In flame of broken dreams
Pray for curses broken
Hope for the Golden Key

Annointed servant
With blessed ability
A raven haired Beauty—
From Heaven's prosperity

6

Cast thy name into the sea
Wounded soul of Love's identity
Eternal wait for blessed healing
My soul's briefest misery

In exile, lost directions flew
Until my purpose was known to me
Thy name into the forgetful sea—
For all eternity.

2nd Assembly

7

The artists pain

Cloaked in sorrows of difficulty

Masks of Agora's Fear

Terror of the dreadful populace

Melodies and verse

Shrouded in mystery

No hope for them who listen—

Who struggle with their misery

Æternal desperation

Neverending flame of desire

Consumes me night and day

In perpetual anguish of ambition

Imprisoned by a New Journey

Bound by a broken dream

A foolish lust of the eyes

Crippling pride of this life

Only Death ends my Odyssey

To see her name in History

An Angel born in Beauty—

In glorious Humility

9

To my beloved Angel
I bid thee last farewell
Fate shall have no mercy
Upon my grief and sorrow

No Raven Haired beauty
To light a dreary world
Death to a Gray Rose
Darkness to this weary soul

Now Destiny's cruelty
Cast thy deception to me!
My fragile heart is broken—
From her beloved Memory

Elizabethan

10

My soul hath wrenched free
In agony she hath departed
Through misery I now go alone
Flailing in chaos and winter cold

No hope, no rest for souls in pain
From tortures laid at my feet
Woman with hair pitched in Ravenwood
In timeless beauty and despair

Lament for the Death of Melody
Greatness buried in cruelty
Wisdom breathed from Heaven's mercy
Lost in eternal Destiny

Words are given through Birth of Fate
Truth now springs from sorrow's bosom
Her heavenly promises hath been delayed
A lifetime of futures is interred

Jonathan Lovejoy

Now terror's regret is fulfilled
When Her soul hath gone from me
My spirit is in unbearable pain—
For all eternity

11

*W*hat glorious days!

When thy purpose is known to me

A Lifetime of hopeless searching

Eternal sea of prophecies killed

Through the darkened haze

Obscured paths are clearly seen

The Light appears in confusion

With fearful possibility

Spirits of Broken Dreams

Perhaps hath deterred in the Hour

Thy mercy flourishes in truth

Grace to an unworthy soul

The Rose hath blossomed to infinity's power

In dreadful ability

A name now glows among the stars—

With immortal predestiny

12

Vast! What strange world I'm in
Where hope echoes with fleeting self worth
Doubt is laced with certainties anew
When spiritual burdens hath lightened away

From whence draweth my total redemption?
As evil treads thy soul's acclaim
Her Light still shines in Heaven's glory
A maiden's promises to fulfill

Since long before the world was formed
Sorrow's grief was given to me
Tomorrow's hope hath wrestled free—
In glorious Humility

13

My spirit bears both love and sorrow
Misery grieves a heart with pain
Haunted flesh endures a distant longing
Indefinable sadness burdens a weary soul

From whence shall thy salvation breathe?
Upon what wind drifts the Day of Peace?
Fate hath shackled me to a mountain
Long months hath drifted into waiting years

Her flame consumes me night and day
Ambitions spring forth as a fountain
Through inadequacy I push forward in fear
Crumbling underneath desire

No confirmation falls from above
In a wilderness I travel alone
Only Her light guides me in darkness—
Shining in this promised land

Jonathan Lovejoy

3rd Assembly

14

Isolated—

Guarded by the Great Flowering Tree

Is the ruin of a dark and tortured past

Dissolved by the years of wind and rain—

Is a house abandoned by Love—

A place now obsolete

Empty—

And desolate for all time

15

Far away—over distant places—
The Winds continue their journey
Across the ocean and mountain ranges
Above every valley and open plain

Forever seeking—
Searching in vain for where to rest—
Finding only places they have already been
The Winds have power over the Earth—
And every inhabitant therein

They could exact annihilation
Were it not for the hand of Fate
Confining them to their endless searching
For a place above the sea

From beyond Olympus comes the west wind
Moving swiftly above the mountains
Across the Black Hills, and great plains of wheat
Unabated to the Appalachian Range

Jonathan Lovejoy

Through the mists of the Blue Ridge Mountains
To the forests and fields of North Carolina
The western breeze moves swiftly along
Raising the dust from harvest fields

Evergreens hold steadfastly
Leaf bearers yield colors to the wind
Leaves twist and swirl to the lonely ground
Mixing with dusts of the farmer's land

Autumn debris blows further eastward
Across the landscape of tobacco country
Beyond fences and unseen boundaries
Into busy lives of women and men—

All Who fail to hear the mournful wail
Blowing through their lives without consequence
They have no concern for the lonely breeze—
The centuries of longing and despair

16

The woman looks up from her mundane duties

Staring across the back yard—

Into the barren field that rests behind their house

She watches the wind become visible—

Given substance—

By a swirling cloud of dust and dirt.

The wind comes across the field—

And into the yard

Until it blows the woman's hair into her eyes.

She wipes the black strands from her face—

And returns to her duties.

She picks up another soaking wet item of clothing—

And hangs it on the clothesline.

The woman is 30 years old—

Partly of Italian heritage

Descended to her through her father.

Her raven hair is shiny and full bodied

Mostly straight—

And lays about her shoulders

And the entire length of her back

Her facial features—
Are what would easily be considered perfect—
Her dark brown eyes are large
And set the correct distance apart
Underneath eyebrows
That are naturally arched to perfection.

Her nose is so blended with her other features
That it would likely go unnoticed—
There are simply no glaring imperfections
Upon its structure or form.
It is neither too small nor too large,
Nor is it pointed, wide or narrow.

It is sized—
Angled and sculpted as a nose should be
As the unheralded—
And indispensably defining feature
Of a woman's natural beauty.

Her lips are pink of their own accord
Unaided by makeup of any kind
As is the smooth, natural tint of her skin.
Her face is unblemished—
Not a single square inch is marked or discolored.

But her eyes have been touched
By the curse of human imperfection—
They are framed by pain and exhaustion
And betray the signs of great physical
And emotional trauma.

The Woman is of average height and weight
Though the dark years—
Have finally begun to take her appetite.
Her ill fitting dress hangs down---
Over a large, pendulous bosom
That has always seemed a bit too heavy for her frame.

Her waist is rather small—
With a cinched, inward curve
That flows outward into rounded, fleshy hips.
She is very embarrassed by her curvy figure
And does her best to wear clothing loose enough—
To hide her shape from view

But her beauty—
Is not the most remarkable thing about her.
In spite of her appearance
There is *no* vanity or self assurance.
She was a shy child and teenager—
And only spoke to her viciously domineering mother.

Some were quick to dismiss the girl as aloof—
Or self important—
While others had been observant enough
To study the look in her dark eyes.
The look of her natural expression—
Is unfathomable.

It immediately arouses pity
Within anyone who notices it.
Reflected in her features
Has always been the depth of Humility—
And genuine naiveté.

Her eyes are filled with empathy and compassion.
Her manner is free of guile—
Deceit—
And natural human duplicity.
Her personality is uncluttered—
By the joyfully narcissistic, self-worshipping conceit
Normally affecting those of great physical beauty.

The Woman's mother had been cruel,
And incredibly abusive.
And the result is a fearful, reclusive woman
With a self image clouded—
With extreme, nearly pathological negativity.

Elizabethan

And locked within that remarkable expression
Is her most defining trait—

It is an indefinable sadness
A profound, distant longing—
For a time when her tortures will end
And when there will be no pain
Nor further cause for fear and dread.

Perhaps, that is why she hears the wind.
Its voice is perceived only by those in mourning,
Whose loneliness is truly epic—
And greater than themselves.

The breeze swirls around her—
Blowing her hair and her dress.
The dead leaves begin to fly down at her
From the giant pecan tree.
A few pecans have already fallen to the ground.
Soon, she will be out here in the yard—
With empty grain sacks—
Filling them with pecans for her husband to sell.
She glances at the gray, furrowed bark of the huge trunk—
And looks up into the branches.

The wind picks leaves from the tree in bunches—
And flings them into the air.
They drift slowly, some falling at her feet—
While others are carried away—

As the wind continues its journey eastward—
Into some other strange, lonely part of the Earth.

The autumn wind suddenly blows again—
Swirling dust into her eyes.
Swirling her long, dark hair into her face.
A flawless countenance.
Miraculously untouched—
And unmarked by the years of torturous abuse.

The wind chills her body—
It warns her of things to come.
It tells her to flee.
To run far away from this place.
But she's too afraid—
And she is in love.
So she chooses not to hear the wind—
Which warns of the sorrows of winter.

The Woman picks up the washtub—
Places it on the back porch—
And goes inside.
Into a house of fear.
Into a house of shadows.

17

He was in a good mood this morning.

He hasn't hurt me since my shoulder healed.

I think maybe he's finally sorry.

He probably won't even whip me anymore.

He kissed me so roughly before he left.

Rougher than he has in a while.

And I don't think he meant to pull my hair that hard.

He just doesn't know how strong he is.

He's been better since my shoulder healed.

He even told me that I shouldn't stay.

That I would be a fool to stay.

But I can't leave—

I can't live without him.

He told me to take good care of myself.

But he was acting so strange…

He acted like he wasn't coming back.

But I know he's coming back.

Because he loves me.

18

*H*e's changing…

Things are so much worse
I think he wants to *KILL* me
I can feel it

He used to feel guilty
He used to be ashamed when he hurt me
He holds back so I'll be well enough to take care of him—
So he can hurt me again when I've healed

The burning was just the beginning
But I won't run…I won't leave him
He can't make me leave—
He can't make me stop caring

But I don't want to die

All I'd have to do
Is show someone the burn scar
And ask them to call the police for me
Then I could get away
But they might put him in jail
I couldn't live with that
I'd rather die than see that happen
I'd rather be *DEAD*

Why does he hurt me all the time?
Are there demons in this house?
Did his mother torture him when he was little?
Did his grandmother?

What's wrong with him?

How much longer can i take the pain?
One day i'll run while its happening, because of the pain
He'll get madder, and he'll catch me
He'll break my leg

He'll set it himself and it won't heal right
I'll limp for the rest of my life
One day, he's going to take a good look at my face
And he's going to beat me in it…

Jonathan Lovejoy

And cut it—
And bite it 'til I can't see
Until i can't feel my face anymore
And then i'll be too *UGLY* to love

Or he'll heat up the knife again
And put out one of my eyes
Just one, so I can see well enough to work
And so I can still please him sometimes

He hasn't smothered me in a long while
He's forgotten about smothering me
He doesn't tie my arms behind my back anymore
And put the pillow over my face—
While he hits me in the stomach

He stopped hitting me with those pieces of wood
He doesn't bite my legs and feet any more
He doesn't punch me in my sides
Or step on my toes with his boots

He hasn't scraped the nails on my back
Or twisted my skin until I had to scream
He hasn't bent my wrists and fingers
Or choked me in a long time

Elizabethan

It's a good thing he likes my face
He never hits me in the face

He used to put nails against my hands and feet
And threaten to nail me to the wall and the floor
He used to threaten to drive tacks into my legs…
He doesn't do any of those things anymore

He hasn't kept food away from me
For a long as i can remember
He lets me sleep in the bed all the time now
It's been months since he locked me out at night

After my shoulder healed
I thought it was all behind us
I thought it was getting better
I thought it was all going to *STOP*

But then, he burned me
I think he used the burn cream because he couldn't help it
Because he couldn't listen to me whimper anymore
But thank God he came back to me

What's going to happen to me now?
After the whipping tonight, what is he going to do?
What part of me is he going to break or burn?
What's going to happen to me tonight?

I want to talk to him,

But i don't know how

I don't know what to say

I get so scared sometimes, i can't breathe—

But I'd rather *DIE* than leave him

I'd rather die

19

I love him—

But I know that I can't stay
After yesterday
I'm not sure that he loves me anymore

I'm afraid
I don't know where to go
I can't tell them that he hurts me
He might get into trouble

I'm not the only one
Plenty of women have to run away
I hope they're not like me
I hope they can get help

I wish I could be brave like other women
Like Momma…
She was strong
No one could have done these things to her

Jonathan Lovejoy

How can I get help,

Without getting him into trouble?

I'll tell them that he MIGHT hurt me

But that he hasn't done it yet

I wish I didn't have to go

I don't want to see anybody

I don't want to talk to anyone

I don't want anyone looking at my ugly face

If only I knew somebody

Somebody who would take care of me

And protect me when he gets angry

I dream about her sometimes

She's like Momma, but different

She's strong, but she loves me

When I wake up

It's like she was really there

I love him—

But I know that I can't stay

4th Assembly

20

Cold autumn breezes begin to blow—
To send premonitions of another winter
When the world will again be interred—
Under a layer of ice and snow

21

*D*ays come and go—

As do the seasons

Until the Earth has made another journey—

And it is Winter again

22

Through the Universe
The Great Meteor came
To signal the last
Of this present age of Men

In Darkness—
And in Gray

Through the decades and centuries—
Lunar dust encircles the Earth
A ring—
Glowing darkness and gray

Now the night sky bears the sign
From the East to the West
As this age is ended
And time ceases to be

23

Lost in the field of mountain snow

The pain of loneliness is interred

While a spirit of epic Love and Beauty

Is bestowed the first fruits of Paradise

24

Eternal night and sorrow creeping

Bewitching eyes of prairie blue

In mournful darkness gently weeping—

But endless hope, forever true

25

In beauty, they walk the Ivy Path
The two of them, disguised in humility
One, with locks pitched in Ravenwood
The other, strands of shimmering Gold

Land of opportunity, halls of privilege
Lives of prestige and comfort
Without a center of morality—
Amoral seeds have blossomed

Immoral seeds will blossom

26

Electric trembling—
A quick upswing. Falling rapidly.
Trembling electric—
Another upswing. Rapid falling.

Energy dancing
Light prancing energetically
Colors bouncing playfully
Blue streaks whirling quiet fury.

Dancing energy sizzling
Lights flowing within
Colors bubbling white—
Streaks twirling again

Lazy lilting uncurls
Hazy tilting
Wilting haze unfurls
Splashed brightness lifting

Elizabethan

Sliding over mountains
Riding downward
Climbing above the clouds
Tumbling quietly

Two, three, until seven
Starfire lights bursting
Waltzing timeless rhythm in heaven
Shimmering ageless rebirth.

Electric trembling—
Tiny upswing. Falling rapidly.
Trembling electric—
Another upswing. Rapid falling.

Glowing nigh unto darkness
Sparkling atmospheres
Flowing high into nighttime
Shimmering stratospheres

Trembling resurrected
Quivering
Explosion restrained—
Contained devastation

Jonathan Lovejoy

Approaching doom impending
Light spinning wildly
Rumbling Creation silently
Earth quaking violently

Two, three, until seven
Thunderous colors blasting
Skies whip into rumbling
Frenzied clamour and cataclysm

Electric trembling…
Lightning!
Sparks falling rapidly…
Darkness

5th Assembly

Jonathan Lovejoy

27

The pirate ship rises in the East
Burning blue and black fire
Searching for a harbour in the peace
Looking for a war to begin

The ship flies carelessly in tune
With Immorality's Evil
Carrying the weapons of mass destruction
Looking for new souls to kill

The ship carries fire above the city
To stares of curious indifference
The bearded warriors are soon revealed
In golden robes of diplomacy

Death is cloaked in fine linen
With intentions shrouded in good will
Devils take their place among men
As Civility threatens eternal sleep

Elizabethan

Now the pirate ship rises in the East
Burning blue and black fire
Searching for a harbour in the peace
Looking for a war to begin

28

At last, thy name is known to me
Birthed in glorious identity
To whence flew my years of misery?
As words appeared from infinity

From ages before the world was formed
This day was forged into my soul
A pinnacle of suffering was laid to rest
As burdens were placed at my feet

From his mercy, the final word was born
An Angel, bathed in Heaven's glory
Crafted by God's immortal spear
With anointed ability

Now future's truth is come to light
In appointed prosperity
Prophecies hath now fulfilled
To a Rose in Humility.

Elizabethan

29

My spirit doth rejoice in awe
Fate hath deemed metamorphosis
A new identity claims this curse
Old sensibilities are dispersed away

The prophet's name is given to me
Delivering words of blessed ability
Showing wisdom of ages infinity
To this dark and evil century

But past fears still plague my soul
Touching me with uncertainty
Sorrow's lifetime hath met defeat
In this Epoch of Victory.

In desperation's hopeless plea
I pray thy name belongs to me
To espouse this word in humility
For all eternity

30

My soul springs forth the truth of ages

Thy name is given in heart's desire

A new release of centuries fears

In due relief from tortured years

Unceasing flow through sorrow's tears

In power hath they ceased to be

To heaven's blessed this glorious gift

In this new identity

31

It pains to recollect tis true

A fine new cloth weaves overdue

In numbers two score and two score and two

With colors craft in every hue

This fine new cloth draped head to shoe

Tis beauty's ways in every view

With joyful days my gladness grew

Until thy winged sadness flew

Spirits depressed have bade adieu

With love and happiness through and through

Now dressed for Impromptu's Rendezvous

This cloth has blessed my joy anew

Jonathan Lovejoy

6th Assembly

32

I saw a city in the clouds
Cloaked in darkness and gray
With cinders blocked in ashen stone
Mortared by raven hearted bone

One rules this city of castle drones
A Prince among powers of the air
Whose countenance bears the face of men
With eyes in colored winter's blue

This prince hath descended down below
Striking fear in hearts of every soul
Craving futures replete with blood and gore
In violence wrought from sea to shore

Fallen angels drift from times before
Thriving upon duplicity
In billowing plumes of fire and smoke
Devastation looms at every door

Elizabethan

I saw a city in the clouds

Cloaked in darkness and gray

With cinders blocked in ashen stone—

Mortared by raven-hearted bone

33

I did a dance in the Dead Room

In a circle of souls in silhouette

From the grave these spirits were shown to me

Laying fear upon which was known to me

One I knew in this realm of life

Took my hand as we gathered 'round

In one unbroken chain of fear

We moved around this demon near

In ignorance I stumbled here

Leaning towards the figure there

Who held the scriptures in never fair

Inticing unsuspecting good

One spirit gripped my hand in fore

Pulling me from Evil's lair

With a smile of life from in Death's door

I thanked this fearful soul to bear

Elizabethan

I did a dance in the Dead Room—
In a circle of souls in silhouette!
From the grave her spirit was shown to me
Laying fear upon which was known to me

34

I

She flung the wicked sword
In the Sargasso Sea
Myra Vanya the Pirate Queen—
Myra the Raven they all knew

A Titan among men, was this Woman of pillage and plunder.
Powers of stone bore every muscle, the wrought of iron in every bone.
Above each plane of every shore, her terror's devastation flew.
Sweeping destruction to misty regions, creeping disruption in souls of men.

Upon these spirits of bravest heart, her dread reputation grew.
'Til women's dreams bore Hellish tears, where echoes screamed unbellished fears.
In flowing hair of Mountain's Pitch, bewitching fair at shoulder's span.
Fire in steely eyes of Blue, four cubits height from crown to shoe—

She flung the wicked sword
In the Sargasso Sea.
Myra Vanya the Pirate Queen.
Myra the Raven they all knew

Elizabethan

II

*T*he early days in evil's reign, they fought to stay the wicked sword.
Whose blade did wield in ice and fire, flamed by cruel terror's youth.
The lass bore witness to Hell's acclaim, demonic plans laid full in due.
Her father stayed the accursed tree, her mother's limbs were borne in two.

Young Raven saw Mother's flesh interred, arms ripped and shorn asunder
As Father gazed in sightless vision, 'til grief crushed his whole heart to naught
Pirates invaded her land of peace, men laid waste to harmony
Choking branches of righteousness, while only their roots doth still remain

Now the tree is known by evil fruit, harvest seeds of pleasure's poison.
The lass was Christened in coals of hate, nurtured in this vengeful flame.
Now through every water of Northern sea, slices three ships of bravery.
From pole to tip of Newfound Worlds, this Pirate Queen is known.

III

*A*cross mountain hamlets to sorrow's home, tomorrow's prophecy is gravely shown
When fury's face hath bravely grown, their hearts hath iced in fear.
Her sword hath sliced the arms of men, as bodies laid upon their cross.
With nails and fervor were many cursed, condemned souls placed upon the hill

The Pirate Queen swept like mighty winds, raiding in the murderers lair.

Clutching them from jails of safety, pierced with nails upon the tree.

These killers did all pray for death, When Myra Vanya took her fearful hold.

Dragged in terror to this Raven Wood, nailed as the Raven calmly stood.

Crosses bore lifted from the earth, sore cries drifted the bloody hour.

Limbs were crushed with agony, repentance sang to stormy skies.

Then Myra Vanya took her fiery blade, slicing through each evil arm.

Leaving flesh nailed to bleeding wood, feeding broken bodies to waiting soil

For one quarter of that medieval century, she treasured the lives of innocence

Despising the flesh of evil men, spilling blood in floods of killing.

Until there blew a fateful storm, above the waters of the deep.

In the clouds they saw the Wrath of Ages, descending from His throne.

IV

As fear took every pirate's soul, they cowered in their ships below.

But one stood firm while voices boomed, perceiving futures where choices loomed

Power drifted from winds of doom, to soothe her dark and fearful spirit.

The fires of vengeance were laid to rest, lifted in this mortal's hour.

Elizabethan

Then Death departed the Pirate Queen, aloft upon the soaring waves,

Fate descended to her mighty soul, a new identity.

Cool Breezes whirled the Raven's hair, the men heard clear her new decree

Then they watched her cast the wicked sword, to the bottom of the briny deep

She bade this past her last farewell

Departing to a peaceful shore

With marriage and righteous lands to dwell

No evil laid this Titan's door

She flung the wicked sword

In the Sargasso Sea

Myra Vanya the Pirate Queen

Myra the Raven they once knew

Jonathan Lovejoy

35

A Spirit from another realm
Whispered utter nonsense to me
Bringing fear to my fragile sanity
Clinging dear to my eternal misery

To me this ghostly voice was clear
Shocking with an evil touch
Blocking myth in truth and such
In darkened times of reason

I hearkened in this lonely season
To a voice of gray and silhouette
The Phantom came from outer darkness
To claim my soul's regret

Knowledge descends in revelation
Demons drift beyond our vision
Devising lust with vile derision
Despising us with Hell's intention

Elizabethan

Now a spirit from another realm
Whispered utter nonsense to me
Bringing fear to my fragile sanity—
Clinging dear to my eternal misery

36

The Queen did marvel her season of death

Cloaked in fine diplomacy

Gazing on a divine reflection

Crowned in golden jeweled perfection

Premonition bloomed in weary days

When perdition loomed in dreary haze

Ceremony hath lost its power

Truth embraced her final hour

The regal soul now takes its flight

Subjects mourn dead flesh interred

Her earthly reign passed interrupted—

When beauty hath at last corrupted

This queen did marvel her season of death

Cloaked in fine diplomacy

Gazing on a divine reflection—

Crowned in golden jeweled perfection

37

Then the hands were dripped with blood and gore

Casting evil eyes to wonder

What manner of wickedness is this

Which tore her sinful nature from her

He split her sex in two

With the blade of fiery contempt

As heaven pitched and roared with thunder—

A witch whore's flesh was torn asunder

38

I saw the Children on the Death Train
Cloaked in ashen gray regret
Though death was not yet known to me
Our train was crashed into the sea

This train tumbled through the mighty deep
In fear I swam harm's evil way
No Children were lifted from their sleep
While they drifted from the light of day

As I walked the shores of eternity
Clouds of doom did loom before me
Children of the train were laid to rest—
At the bottom of the briny deep

I saw the Children on the Death Train
Cloaked in ashen gray regret
Though death is not yet known to me—
Their train is buried beneath the sea

7th Assembly

Jonathan Lovejoy

39

In misery he hopes for a better life

Without the pain of fear and sorrow

A softspoken man of great kindness—

And greater humility

72

40

A Monkey with a Gun
Looked to have a little fun
So he jumped from the tree
So the other animals could see

Then the monkey with the gun
Rooked a crooked looking run
The monkey took his gun
And shot a cat just for fun

He ran back to his tree
So the other cats wouldn't see
But the cat had a son
Who found the monkey with his gun

Then the kitten shot the gun—
Into the monkey just for fun

41

Accursed fruit of my mother's tree
Winged lust departs upon wings of eagles
Flowers drift from trees into spring breezes
Wafting into the houses of immorality's evil

Accursed fruit of my mother's tree
Singing dust from the throat of her privileged days
Showers have lifted from these gray clouds of sorrow
There is no rest for her weary soul

Her soul possesses my dark and fearful spirit
For each and every turn of season
I give neither rhyme nor foolish reason—
For her stygian ways of killing

42

The Angel of Death appeared in dread

Though he hath no power to give

He said to me "Though you be dead…"

"Yet shall you also live."

Jonathan Lovejoy

8th Assembly

43

I've heard them sing of sunny days

They often seem too far away

Now the future rains from Hosanna's Way

Singing joy's refrain in the Autumn Day

44

The Queen of Happiness ruled the land
'Til every woman was in her hands

They were impressed by this Queen of Happiness
From her wealth and riches she wore a smile of joyfulness
With stealth she scored a place in history's lore
In good health she bore this reputation of cheerfulness

The women laid themselves at her throne of loveliness
They bade their sanity ado with aggression
This queen worked them into a whirlwind of tears
Their years of pain swirled into a vortex of cheers

Her charisma worked the magic of heart's desire
Her power jerked the women from the edges of reason
In every season she saw her wealth and riches grow—
As the women sacrificed their whole lives with fire

The Queen of Happiness ruled the land
'Til every woman was in her hands

Jonathan Lovejoy

With violence they defended this dear Queen of Happiness
With savagery they abandoned their dream of clear mindedness
With fury they pledged to love a world of fake joyfulness
With rage they gave themselves over to lasciviousness

This queen stood and watched her hoardes of legion
She marveled as they wept tears in every region
Refusing to let them see the truth of ages
As she pondered tomorrow's flood of joyful rages

As she pondered her millions and billions of wages

Now, they worshipped this Queen of Happiness with fervor…
Feeding upon the violent frenzy of emotion
Until they suppressed their excesses of depression—
Buried deep into their recesses of repression

45

There's a stidgey widget in my gidget
Said the cricket to the crow
Then the crow looked back at him
And said "you have to go"

There's a stidgey widget in my gidget
Said the cricket to the bear
Then the bear looked back at him
And chased him from his lair

There's a stidgey widget in my gidget
Said the cricket to the whore
Then the whore looked back at him
And shoed him out the door

There's a stidgey widget in my gidget!
Said the cricket to the man
But then the man looked back at him—
And smashed him with a can

46

This man had seen two score and ten
Fifty years old his wife and he
The wife drifted off to sleep again
The man gazed into his TV

In a haze he flipped from trash to taste
Through the maze of boredom he made his haste
Until his eyes went wide with wonder
When teenage thighs were spread asunder

Do you want my sex old man?
Are there things you wish you could do to me?

His video girl in golden hair
Hurled this sin with skill and flair
Her skin beaded wet with sweat so fair
Her eyes pleaded lust from evil's lair

Elizabethan

The man watched this busty music girl
Quicken his heart with thrust and twirl
As devil beats came forth in tow
The man felt his resurrection grow

But the wife did lift her eyes from slumber
Inquiring of the whorish number
The man turned off his body's game
And bade farewell his schoolgirl flame

Jonathan Lovejoy

9th Assembly

47

Two souls adrift in the evil land
Rode their chariot of poverty
They came upon the dining stand
Dressed in clothes of misery

They stood in hopeless anticipation
Mocked with merciless derision
Waiting in the filthy station
Torn by fearful indecision

Man and Wife were judged in ridicule
With stares and whispered cruelty
Tormented by others with evil rules
Of human impropriety

Now these two departed the evil land
In their chariot of poverty
They left the dreary dining stand—
Dressed in clothes of misery

48

A woman looked into a mirror
To see what there was to see
Locks of gray and white with silver
Where dark hair used to be

She bade farewell to youthful days
For all eternity

But Love still walked the winding road
Beneath the Flowering Tree
Her Love did walk the winding road—
In a place above the sea

In a land beyond the sea

49

Their evil is forever hidden
Partakers of every sin forbidden
Their father's curse is born
Their mother's sinful blood is born

Wicked youth shall never prosper
A mother's life of vice has cost her
A recompence is due
Her vile comeuppance is overdue

Children of an evil mind
Become adults alike in kind
To make the world regret
They make the wicked world forget

A sinful father is laid to rest
A sinful mother shall curse her breast
That nursed their evil dawn
She nursed their accursed devil spawn

Elizabethan

This mother's soul is thrown to Hell
Because she let the evil dwell
In her son's corrupted soul—
In her daughter's twisted wicked soul

A world is plunged to darkest night
Because no guide for wrong and right
Was given to her son—
Her daughter's sin is never done

50

The Red Fly came by and bye

To tell us all what dark and ruesome manner we should die

When the Red Fly comes by

All of us will die

All of us will cry and cry

When living eyes are told what gruesome manner we will die

When the Red Fly comes by

All of us will die

51

*T*was kept outside the promised land
To watch the world fall hopelessly in love with the Cookie Man
My fate was planned
Before the Earth began

Beware this silken Cookie Man
Whose touch is such that gold falls from the sky into his hands
His fate was planned
Before the Earth began

We were held outside this promised land
Compelled as they all fell into the spell of the Cookie Man
Our fate was planned
Before our birth began

52

Violence gripped these women in full
Tearing through their Beauty
In silence I saw their lust for blood
Blossom to maturity

One with raven locks of coal, swearing through her beauty.
Spitting venom to the other maiden, whose hair was golden as the sun—
The blonde took hold of the brunette's mane, 'til humiliation was wrought through tears
The Raven sought to have fought her fears, 'til the Maiden crushed her pride to naught

I sat trembling in my Chariot of Death
Waiting for the flash of light

The Raven broke free from the Maiden's ire, to flee into the Ivy House.
The Maiden followed her with fire, pulling her from the privileged house.
The blonde took hold of brunette's mane, pulling at her sanity.
She drug the Raven to the lawn, slicing at her dignity.

Elizabethan

I watched her claw the Raven sore, through indignant screams of mercy
But the Maiden could summon no compassion, exacting cold revenge with passion
At last, the brunette rose to feet, to escape the fury in blonded beauty
The Maiden watched the Raven flee, to her upper room of bonded duty

But then the stuff of witches brew
Manifested upon the lawn
The Raven returned with a rod of iron
To point it at the Maiden's life—

I sat trembling in my Chariot of Death
Waiting for the flash of light

She drew the screams from the Maiden's mouth, she sat upon the Maiden's breast
She placed the rod against her head, she threatened to do the firing pin
The Maiden screamed for absolution, staring at the rod of iron
The Raven beamed with satisfaction, feeding upon the Fear of Death

But at last this evil braved its course
Through these two daughters of privilege
They returned into their House of Ivy
As though no wickedness was done

Violence gripped these women in full
Tearing through their Beauty
In silence I saw their lust for blood—
Blossom to maturity

Jonathan Lovejoy

10th Assembly

53

Gone in ever waiting soil

This ne'er do well was laid to rest

Forever laid to rest in waiting soil

This ne'er do well

54

Life has burned a hole in me

Good things are forever gone from me

I rest weary in the curse of years—

I embrace my dreary season of Death

55

What a curious sensation it might be
To digest a morsel inside of me
If sustenance is never bore—
These hunger pains shall rend me sore

What a curious sensation it will be
To digest this morsel inside of me

56

BIRDS flew under Cloak of Night

Drowning in the darkened rain

I gazed into this darkened rain

Amazed by what there was to see

I saw a sea of chirping song

Hearken from infinity

I saw a sea of chirping song

Extended to eternity

From among this endless flock of night

There arose a single bird in flight

One giant creature in my sight

With feathers pitched in raven's blood

Through the flood of rain this giant flew

In too great a winged girth to know

This bird hovered near the Earth below

Drifting to the ground below

Jonathan Lovejoy

I ran through my nightmare House of Tears
Other windows showed this darkened rain
The creature met my frightened stare
Stalking towards my House of Fear

Birds flew under cloak of night
Drowning in the darkened rain
I saw a sea of chirping song
Hearken from infinity—

I saw a sea of chirping song
Extended to eternity

11th Assembly

57

From whence cometh forth your grief and sorrow
From what shores were thy miseries wrought
Under what dark and heavy cloud wast thou born
What stormy sky delivered thee to this accursed world

From where draweth thy eternal redemption
From whence doth thy salvation breathe
Under which cloud doth evil lay
Waiting to be born

Elizabethan

58

As a woman looked helplessly from the sky

Her daughter turned into a butterfly

It flew into a spider's den

Her daughter was never alive again

59

In ships from space and technology

With childlike appeal to our psychology

The little creatures left the whole earth in awe

With their unique physiology

These creatures descended upon the earth

Beings of mass irresistibility

Miniature two legged extraterrestrials

With charismatic ability

These creatures descended upon the earth

With malevolent sensibility

Elizabethan

60

Why did the white fish swim to me?
I saw it struggle 'til it was free
It moved in Glory to where I lay
Flowing fear into my darkest day

The white fish breathed the air I breathe
On fins of beauty it moved away

On wings of beauty it flew away

Jonathan Lovejoy

12th Assembly

61

The Great Bull Calf came down from the sky
Running full across the open plains
The great bull snorted his angry cry
Craving his beloved land of rain

Earth cattle stood half his massive girth
Five cubits spanned from hoof to crown
The bull searched in vain for his star of birth
Shrieking terror through the provincial town

The women screamed from behind the doors
The children's nightmares had come to fore
The men prayed that there would be no wars—
With this creature from the distant shore

But fate had mercy upon their soul
When the calf was called from this earthly mire
They watched it run as thunder rolled
Blazing a trail of dust with fire

Elizabethan

The calf gazed back towards the sky
Running full across the open plains
The great bull snorted his angry cry
Returning to the land of rain

62

What glorious day can this be?

His promise comes forth from the clouds

Heaven's promise brings forth mercy

Upon Earth's brief immortality

When colors hath breathed from the clouds—

From His glorious infinity

63

The great ship lies above the waiting soil
A place to brave the Judgment Sea
Above the rising mountains of the east—
They drifted into history

The fountains of the deep broke free to the sky
Til every eye beheld His fury
The rains fell upon this face of the beast
Til every wicked breath was ceased to be

Winds flew in quarters of the earth
Lifting waters from the mighty deep
They saw Heaven revealed in the clouds—
Colors of a Divine promise to keep

Above the rising mountains of the east
They drifted to rest in history
Now the great ship lies beneath the waiting soil
The Ark that braved the Judgment Sea

64

The Idols gazed into the yard

To ponder hard their magic card

Their tombstone's message will not be heard—

Where other Idols now rest interred

13th Assembly

65

I wonder where it is they go

Those children who are trapped in tears upon the Plane of Death

I have seen their faces before they go

The eyes go dark

The nostrils then become holes in their pretty faces

Their teeth grow large while skin moves away from their mouth and other places

I marvel at their skeleton faces

When the pain they feel is shown to me

It seems that few have ever been allowed to really see

Then I know

That they must go

That they must board this plane I see

That they must travel until they have flown far away from me

I wonder where it is they go

Those children who are trapped in tears upon the Plane of Death

Have you seen their faces?

Before they go?

Elizabethan

66

My mind doth burn with my heart's pain

As gray clouds reclaim a weary soul

67

They pinned their hopes to the UFO
Upon a ride among the stars and fire
To hide inside the comet's veil
To Heaven's trail they do aspire

For Heaven's Veil they do aspire

Their desire rests with eternity
Where earth gleams a distant memory
They dream of trips beyond this world
Where joyfulness becomes reality

World weariness grips in spirit strife
Dreariness grieves their souls to weep
Until they leave this light of life
Kissed by Infinity's night of sleep

They pinned their hopes to the UFO
To Heaven's trail they do aspire—

For Heaven's Veil they do aspire

Elizabethan

68

As I roamed the halls of luxury
The thief in black pointed death to me
Saying "Thou shalt not live to procreate"
Prepare thyself to die

Terrors devastation grew
While the points of death flew all around me
As the man in black pointed death at me—
I prepared myself to die

69

No language breathed with flair

No words bequeathed in roses fair

Will soothe the fires of misery

Burning within my soul

70

What is this I hear

The mail carrier's steps are fading

Her letter hath clicked inside the metal house

What is this—

The letter has come!

Tonight—

I may collect it

This night

I shall recollect it

71

Hello, Little World!

I see your pretty flowers unfurled

White butterflies play in flight

Little hummingbirds fly in my sight.

But Spring has gone away

And now Summer is here to stay.

Hello, Little Cat!

I see you asleep on that mat.

You'd better open your eye

Before a little mouse wanders by

So many naps every day

When will you wake up to play?

Hello, Little Bug!

I see you creeping over that rug.

By your colors I can see

A ladybug in front of me.

Now hurry out, so you can fly—

Underneath the beautiful blue sky.

Elizabethan

Hello, Little Pup!
I see you knocking over my cup.
We spilled milk on the floor
And now there isn't any more.
There's no room in here to run
Let's go outside to have fun.

Hello, Little Bee!
I see you looking at me.
Buzzing around all day,
With all work and no play.
Making your honey so sweet
For me and all my friends to eat.

Hello, Little Rose!
I see your beauty that grows.
In red, pink or white
You're the prettiest flower in sight.
But are those colors I see
The only colors you can be?

Hello, Little Worm!
I see you wriggle and squirm.
Crawling slowly all around,
Always hiding in the ground.
You come out now and then—
But when will I see you again?

Jonathan Lovejoy

Hello, Little Tree!
I see how tall you will be.
High and green you will grow
Like all the other trees I know.
In your shade, I will rest
While songbirds sing and nest.

Hello, Little Frog!
I see you on top of that log.
All day and night long,
I hear you croaking your song.
But I wonder where you go
When winter winds begin to blow?

Hello Little Fish!
I see you moving with a swish
You were near shore just before
But now I can't see you anymore.
In this pond, or in the sea
You're always too far away from me.

Hello, Little Bird!
I hear you singing to be heard
In the sky, or in a tree
Your voice is music to me
But why can't you ever stay
When the daytime goes away?

Elizabethan

Hello, Little Cloud!
I see you floating with a crowd
Across the blue Summer sky
Every shape is going by
You're so fluffy and white—
I wish I could see you at night.

Hello, Little Star!
I see how far away that you are.
Shining bright in the sky—
Your light always catches my eye.
But where is it you go
When the sunlight begins to glow?

Hello, Little Sheep!
I see you jumping in my sleep
Now help me hurry to dream
Of cake and strawberry ice cream
Today was a good day for me—
The world is a lovely place to be

72

Chariots of sweet mercy are in my sight

Blazing with the fires of Heaven

73

My soul has built a defense against the cold

Somewhere…

In the shadows of warmth

The cold is only a distant memory

Jonathan Lovejoy

74

I sing the praise of a rainy day

When joy descends from Heaven's Way

14th Assembly

75

The girl in red
Is limping, they said
She'll never make it
To the end of the road

The girl in red
Is dead, they said
They found her body—
At the end of the road

76

I saw an alien in the skylight
In the rains that fell from the crimson night

I endeavored to fight—
But my screams were held by the demon's might
He used his gaze with eerie spite
To grip my spirit tight

Thunder rolls through creation
Lightning tears the sky in two
The raindrops fall upon my skin
As I ponder how I will die tonight

The rains are falling from the twilight
I am held immobile by a fearful sight
I see an alien in the skylight
Feeding upon my fright

77

Death descended upon her face
The woman with every reason to live
With reluctance she slowed her hectic pace—
So she could have more life to give

Sweet words are laced with bitter venom
As she grinned a phony smile at me
Pulling me to her evil breast
Despising my days of poverty

Psalms of love bear man's duplicity
Prayers breathed from their spirit of audacity
From her soul she screamed to darkened skies
Spitting poison into my eyes

Her claws burned hot with fires of lust
Her teeth dripped cold with stings of hatred
Her lips swore my body to the dust
Her heart bore damnation for my soul

Elizabethan

Then Death descended to her face
This woman with every reason to live
With fervor she kept her hectic pace
Til she had no further life to give

78

A woman in white drifted through my door
Pointing a crooked finger
She said, "though Death hath naught for thee,"
"Despair and pain will linger"

I saw her throw a golden sphere
With awe my soul grieved cold in fear

The woman did throw the sphere at me
With terrible intention
It touched me with a pestilence
Too horrible to mention

This woman in white sent a golden sphere
Into my soul's dimension

79

A woman claimed knowledge of my history
To lure me to her House of Tranquility
This lady remained a mystery
Her eyes bore serpentine duplicity

Through kind and courteous inquiry
I bade again my family's tree
She said "Cast thy worries into the sea"
"I have a photograph for thee"

I gazed upon the Tides of Lore
Eyes of gray and misery
A photograph from days of yore
Captured lives of poverty

"Original Sin" she said to me
A voice kissed with purposes of dire intention
Noises hissed with demonically inspired invention
Too fearful for comprehension

Jonathan Lovejoy

Knowledge of grief was laid upon me
She said "Death shall be required of thee"
I perished with knowledge of my History
Accursed fruit of my mother's tree

I died inside her evil house
Devoured by Serpentine Duplicity

15th Assembly

80

The witch told her daughter to pick the switch
The girl asked her mother which switch to pick
The woman said "you bitch, you know which switch is which"
"The one that will cut your white skin to blood"

Through the flood of rain the daughter found her switch
At the ditch by which the razor switches grew
Though the mud she walked back to her cabin of pitch
Where the woman itched to make her witch's brew

Thunder rolled as she handed her mother the switch
Then she cried while the witch cut her skin to blood

Elizabethan

81

How does this man formulate his plan?

The crocodiles are in his power

Alligators, snakes and lizards flee

While the people ponder his wizardry

Jonathan Lovejoy

82

Upon a time long ago, in a Land Beyond the Sea
Melodies sang from a Whispering Tree
Far away places near gathered 'round
To marvel this miracle in Heavenly sound

From summer's hour, warm winds would whirl
To swirl precious harmonies in righteous pearl
Every eye did blink from wonders saw
While leaves played symphonies to wondrous awe

Pause ruled peaceful in the Land of Knee
Happiness because of their Whispering Tree
Through centuries they came in blade and fire
Burning, slicing with Wicked's Ire

Not an inch of wood, nor a scrape of green
No harm from witches or terror's glean
Warlords and Beasts and Wizards flee
From Summer's leaves of Melody

Elizabethan

In Autumn's hour, enchanted hymn
Silences by Nature's whim
To colors flamed in every hue
From Crimson Red to Harvest Blue

Now Winter's gale through courses blow
To bury their land in Ice and Snow
Every leaf 'tis white as Luna's Light
Bright until their Spring's Delight.

As Winter claimed the Land of Knee
The Queen did marvel her Whispering Tree
From root to crown was white as Snow
To guard her world from conquering foe

When Spring interred fair Winter's cold
Their snowy tree spun leaves of Gold
Dear Legend cried both far and near
Hear Splendor's season in Beauty's year

Now Creation breathed warm Summer's breeze
When life seeks shelter beneath the trees
The golden leaves hue green in glee
While their Tree of Life sings a Melody

83

A color veil whirled among the stars
Swirling the night's infinity
The veil encircled into a sphere
Lifting my unresisting fear

It drifted from the sky above
Resting in the land before me
In fear I watched this Heaven's Light
Bring beauty to this evil shore

Its colors grieved upon the Earth
Its spirit moved through this Valley of Shadows
No souls gave heed of this glorious light
Redemption for the hearts of men

These colors encircled into a sphere
Lifting to the night's infinity
Now the color veil whirls among the stars
Drifting from lost humanity

84

They pledged their future to a pentium god
Forged in prophecies of three score and four
Wisdom died upon their thirst for knowledge
Hope dissolved in poisoned lust for reason

Blinded by sin and carnality
Imprisoned by their soul's immorality
They languished in darkened clouds of wickedness
Choking upon their season of death

Accursed seed of Creation's Garden
Corrupted fruit from Divinity's Tree
Evil blight upon their native soil
Waiting for their Judgment Day

Men pledged their future to a new divinity
Forged in prophecies of fear
With nightmares of eschatology
Borne from their beloved technology

85

AWoman of Beauty set misery upon the Earth

Disguised as harmless diversion

Ingenuity's evil captured my eye

When geniality traversed into subversion

This Beauty set evil into the sky

To submerge our souls into perversion

I confronted this woman fearfully

Juna was the name she spoke to me

A face covertly, incontrovertibly sunny—

A voice replete with sweetest milk and honey

The woman stared necromantically

She said "This world shall not escape from me"

I perceived again her wicked name

As she vanished for shores from whence she came

Elizabethan

This Woman of Beauty set misery upon the Earth

Disguised as a costless diversion

Accursed days of my mother's birth

When hope was lost to perversion

Jonathan Lovejoy

16th Assembly

86

Heaven is what I see

Heaven is what I feel

Heaven is in the clouds above me

What is in the Earth Below—

Evil is what I see

Evil is what I feel

Evil is in the world before me

What is in this world before me?

Elizabethan

87

I chose not this profession
Rather it chose me
Yet no word had been given
Until age thirty three

A failure in life
At age thirty three
At age thirty three

Labouring through accursed
Inadequacy
Relinquished to this burden
Of obscurity

88

Withhold not thy blessing from this unworthy servant!
Open Heaven's gate to rain prosperity
Upon my weary days of waiting—

Let peace shine as the shimmering diamond's light!
Let golden sheaves rise upon these hills—
And mountains of my despair!

Fulfill beauty's promise within me
Open these dreary doors of difficulty
Stay this cold hand of cries and misery—
Let thy bounties rest in this land before thee!

89

Fate decides over reason

Destiny overrides indecision

For where the will of man ends—

God's Will begins

And one cannot change what is meant to be

Fate is a river

Flowing to an eternal sea—

The Sea of Destiny

90

The girls were all catty

With cruelty

They said "fatty fatty boomalatty"

"You're too fat for me"

Fatty fatty boomalatty

You're too fat for anybody

17th Assembly

Jonathan Lovejoy

91

A Kitten with a Gun
Itched to have a little fun
So she jumped from the tree
So the other kittys could see

Then the Kitten with the gun
Slicked a wicked kitten run
Then Miss Kitty took her gun
And shot a cat just for fun

She ran back to her tree
So the other kittys could see
Then the kitten shot her gun
Into her head just for fun

92

Years removed from claws
Clutches of evil strength and power
Haunted still by ghosts of darkness
Seeking claim to a mind and soul

One in bitterness and regret
With disdain for the ones she bore
Taking solace in her sorrow bed
Saying "Child, I have no use for thee."

The other in rage and lack of sanity
Hiding in wait, lurking
Hearing the child's voice in pleading
Calling from another realm

The child hears footsteps from the Angry One
Thumping the darkened halls
Pounding fear into his soul
Sounding terror in the air around him

Jonathan Lovejoy

The child sees the shadow

Emerge from outer darkness creeping

Rounding the corner into the gray room

Saying "I have no use for thee"

Shadows conspire

United plans of destruction

One with weapons of icy neglect

The other, weapons of fire and pain

Years from accursed fruit of their labour

One who writhes in poverty

The other in the torment of death…

Haunting

93

I glided to a desert place
Braving cold and isolation
Searching for the man to tell me where I should go in this accursed life

I gazed upon his bearded face
This master of the craft I seek
Waiting for him to tell me where I should go in this accursed life

As we engaged the Rules of Ability
I knew I would master the craft I seek
But still unknowing of where it is I should go in this accursed life

I rest alone in this desert place
Braving cold and isolation
Wondering…

94

I curse the witch who bore me
i spit on the grave of the devil who beat me sore

Accursed days of my wicked birth
one who writhes in poverty
another who writhes in the torment of death
i pray for their eyes to shrivel into seeds

Seeds giving birth to worms of pain
burrowing deep in their evil brain
until they breathe eternity's scream
torturing their dreams for infinity

Them who pull my bloody form
from a place of warmth and safety
to thrust me to a Valley of Fear
a place of twilight and darkened silhouette

I curse the witch who bore me
i spit on the grave of the devil who beat me sore

95

I searched the ground
I searched the air
I searched high and low for the rocks of color
Painted every purest color in the rainbow

Earth stone more precious than silver and gold
More precious than diamonds
More rare than every treasure in the mighty deep
Fairer than every pearl of the darkened sea

I searched the ground
Having found the earth rocks of color
Having value to not a single soul but me
I would exchange these precious stones—
For the chance to know my destiny

A thing more rare than treasures of the deep
Fairer than pearls of the darkened sea

96

There is a story to be told

This, of a mountain girl...

A girl who can never grow old

She drifts upon the mountain breeze

Enshrouded beauty

A wisp of willow in the mountain forest trees

Lifting the breath of every season

Strolling through the mists of nature's warmest evening song

There was a girl of fifteen, fairer than day

Hair blacker than the blackest night

When she was twelve, sickness came to her mountain cabin

Claiming the life from her sister and her brother

Then the pestilence took her poppa away

Until at last... her mother and only she were left alone

Her time was 1834

The year she became forever young was 1834

Elizabethan

But three years before, she was but a girl of twelve
Joyful, kind, loving her mother, working their vegetable land
Together they owned a log house—
And one single acre of ground

But in that planting season
When the father laid in waiting soil
They saw no land of plenty
And no days of prosperity

Even so, the girl had her mother
Whom she loved every bit as dearly

Soon, another sickness came to their cabin paradise
But of a sort unseen in the body
This took her mother's mind with grief
Until it devoured her fragile sanity

They braved another unfruitful harvest
Languishing their winter season
But the girl stayed by her mother—
Unaware of how deep this illness had grown

One night, in her fifteenth year,
Under the summer light of the brightest moon—
The mother called her from her sleeping bed…
She escorted her loving daughter deep into the forest wood

Jonathan Lovejoy

There, in the fickle lunar light
She brandished her sharpened blade
And she stabbed her daughter in shrieks and screaming
Over and over, until she screamed no further scream

Until her life's red blood was gone
And she left her lovely daughter there alone
And her daughter could not ever know
Where it is her mother had gone

The mother drifted quietly…
Over the brown forest needle floor
Searching for the silver light
Of the summer mountain moon

She saw the light in the clearing
Shining brightly above her cabin of pitch
She entered her tomb as the living
Brandishing the blade upon herself

Until she was forever dead—
To life's torment and war

In isolation, her body was found by a kindly soul
Who lamented her tragic bravery
And buried her along with the rest of her beloved family
But the whereabouts of the girl were never known—

Elizabethan

Her time was the year of a comet—
When she became forever young in 1834

And bye and bye
Whenever a mountain train passed on a summer's night
Sparks would fly—
As the train wheels were screeched to a fiery cry

When the engineer stalled his speeding train
To an appalling, shrieking cry
The sight of the bright figure
Caused such a dreadful fright

The train squealed to a halt, the lights flickered off
And the passengers were left chattering in the dark
Some screamed when the gray figure made of moonlight
Stepped lightly through the train

Peering at them with curious eyes of sorrow
Searching among them…
Wondering where it is
That her beloved mother could have gone

But this train no longer climbs these mountain slopes
There is no traveling path among these hills
The modern train rides somewhere down
And far away below

Somewhere, apart from the ghostly echo of this mystery
They know nothing of this old history—
The lost story of this mountain girl
Who wanders through the sorrow of her death

Searching for where it is
That her beloved mother could have gone

In long, straight locks of dark'ned hair
She drifts upon the mountain breeze
Enshrouded beauty—
A wisp of willow in the mountain forest trees

Lifting the breath of every season
Brightest in the summer season
Strolling through the mists
Of nature's warmest evening song

But her little story can never be told
This, of a mountain girl…
A girl who can never grow old
A girl who became forever young in 1834

Now she is forgotten, forever lost—
In everlasting days of mountain lore

18th Assembly

97

*W*hat is this I feel?
This sickness, coursing through my body
Is this Death?
Stealing strength from my arms
Drawing energy from my legs of power

Shall I not awaken from this dark place
To never again see the Light of Day
But the angel hath said
"Thou hast no infirmity…you shall not die"

Though my body cries out for the grave
I shall not die

Elizabethan

98

A man came to me
In profound ambiguity
Saying "I have a brick for thee"
For thy accursed foundation

Compounding my uncertainty
Confounding my sensibility

99

The words of omission

When magic asks to be seen by the light

When the light is asked by magic to breathe

Whenceforth does your fearfulness arise

In these times there is no peace

Unto the wicked borne under the sun

Then there is action

A reason to live

100

Melodies call from a distant place

Harmonies from beyond the sea

Phrases of such sublime beauty

As never before were wrought before me

Voices of instruments

Colors of wood and string

Brass tones

Winds of purest velvet

Ingenuity breathed from Jubilee

Old voices of originality

Lifting my soul aloft—

Drifing upon clouds of every season

101

*Y*ellowed with the dust of years
Tears of this day's obscurity
Fears of times and brutal seasons
Upon these souls of mourning

Harshness, intensity
Drowning in a twilight of reason
Angry currents of adjacency
Upon which direction these courses flew

Avalon!
Where do thy citizens succumb!
When radicals give birth to death
Thy Hellish days hath come to fore
Thy shore of happiness has come to naught

Elizabethan

102

I see it passing through

There, among the trees and leaves of color—

Winds whispering of less glorious times

Days of torture

Agony, pain and suffering

Wafting among the oakwood trees

Sufferings untold, unknown screams of history

Times of killing and bloody sleep

Revenge

Cold and deep

Jonathan Lovejoy

103

A spring tree in waiting

Is my heart indeed

A soul's winter pain

Has laid claim in misery

The waiting tree

Has no solace from days of living

No rest from a weary path chosen

No sleep for a burdened spirit

A spring tree in waiting

Has no leaves of summer's tears

Spring's hour hath no power to shine—

Upon this day of fear

Elizabethan

19th Assembly

104

From the distance

I hear the train bells ringing

Singing of my approaching death

It has come for me

I can hear the chiming of the whistle train

Whose refrain is the voice of pain itself

Shrieking the agony of souls

The solace of my soul's domain

105

In this hour of my darkest season

The brightest rain falls in power

When there is no reason to travel onward

Blessings loom from stormy skies

And the voice of heaven cries my redemption

As I am nigh to a lonely grave

I brave these troubled times of strife

In a life renewed in my darkest day

Having prayed for this blessed reprieve from bondage

My answer hearkens from the evening day

When the brightest rain falls in hope and power

Devouring my every sorrow away

Jonathan Lovejoy

106

Melodies resound the Great Music Hall

Above the river valley of No Where's Land

Harmonies pour down a crystal waterfall

To nourish the Valley of Cerulean Sand

Heaven's might beams from a darkened sky

Above the Players of Orchestra's Light

As their dreams wish where mountain eagles fly

Souls are redeemed by this otherworldly sight

Whispering peace in the fields of plenty

By the river valley of a distant land

To this new world I have traveled alone

To walk these Shores of Azurean Sand

107

Joy springs from Sorrow's Bosom
To light a path though the darkened place
The land of evil and wicked's throne
Stands as a mountain before me

Faith hath defeated the beast
To cast him to the Bright Land Sea
A netherworld of his regret
For my soul's eternity

108

Azure eyes of bluest sky
Hair as gold as the mountain sun
Skin as white as the brightest day
Lips the color of crimson

Her cheeks are as lovely as the rose
Her nose is sculpted with angel's flair
The fairest maiden to abound—
In this valley of shadow and silhouette

109

My time has come

The Raven will pick my bones clean

My hour of deliverance is at hand—

My war with evil is not won

On the shores of Heaven

I will see soothing days

A time of peace

A reprieve from the place of living

O glorious death!

Let not thy sting cause pain to my flesh

Let not thy poison cast fear into my soul

Withold not thy blessing from me

On the shores of Heaven

I will see soothing days

Relief from the pain

Of this firelight

110

Answers conceal the blocks of light
Symbols reveal the meaning of life

From the caves of spite three wishes thrown
Tapestries woven in Harvest Loom
Doomful promises disperse the night
When golden mysteries are clearly shown

This page turns upon the Thief of Blight
Hearkened above this spirit strife
A foreshadow of destiny's enlightened shore
Boldly near the crowning throne

When answers reveal the blocks of light
Symbols conceal the meaning of life

20th Assembly

111

*C*ruel Fate!

Why must thou mock me?

Images fall from above

To confound the gates of reason

This may be a Season of Plenty

But how can this be known?

Thou has hearkened unto cruelty

Where this servant lives unawares

Bless this house with Truth

Bestow revelation upon me

Cease thine mockery of this weary soul

Upon this hour of peace

112

When I saw that the world was gone
The smoke was blacker than black
Like a cloud of oil
Billowing towards the sky

Orange flames below it were small
Devoured by inky black smoke
Looming high

When I saw that the world was gone
The smoke was as thick as black liquid
As high as a mountain
As poisonous as Death

113

Perceptions inspire dreadful fright

When blood drips down from Crimson Light

No man hath seen the Thief of Blight

Escaped from the pit of burning light

Where tortured dreams antagonize

Where poison stings to agonize

Where burnings ravage non seeing eyes

Where evil seeks no fool's disguise

Perceptions inspire dreadful fright

When blood drips down from Crimson Light

114

Wishes are like dreams

Fading upon wings of sleep

Carried aloft to mountain highs

Where beauty fades to Terra's Calling

Voices cascading white and snowy peaks

Wishes…

Unfulfilled in this life

Substance for souls who have departed

Dreams are like wishes…

Unfulfilled in this life

Jonathan Lovejoy

115

*B*lack! You never wrote me back!

We can't have no knack

Cacky lack like that

No wacked knacky cack

Siddle dack like that

Fiddle Faddle Fat

Cat diddle daddle like that

Black?

You never wrote me back!

184

21st Assembly

116

Peace can find no slumber

When ghosts roam the halls of luxury

Fear doth overtake thee

Although no phantom's voice is heard

But thy skin pricks with tingling

A tickling inclination for flight

Seek not to find the Keys of Life

Among these treasures of evil strife

117

The witness, the prophet

The Queen for a Day

Mourn for souls laid at their feet

The grass, the leaf

The fairy in the tree

Cry for souls laid at their feet

118

We followed the Golden Wheel
High into the mountain snow
Down the white and brightened slopes
Far across the lighted plain

The wheel leads onto winding roads
Underneath the Great Flowering Tree
Through green forest trees of Summer's Life
We followed behind the wheel

We carried forth bravely
Until my power, my force of life gave way
Giving heed to no revival
Having no more heart that I survive

The Wheel continued its oddysey
Somewhere in the Land of Knee
Beyond my grieving vision
Moving to my destiny

Elizabethan

I can not follow the Golden Wheel
When my life force is taken from me
I am helpless
Hopeless

Fate leaves me abandoned
Left stranded on this Road to Freedom
A place I shall not see in joy
When my force of life is gone

119

*S*ome thoughts will fade

And cower from Lucid's Glare

There they flourish in the dark of Shade

In the place where dreams are made

As I lay grieving at Death's Door

She drifted to me under cloak of night

As I lay breathing in the bosom of pain

She came to me in Fires of a Dream

From across dark and misty plains

She reached above the Winds of Time

Finding the core of my soul's agony

Infusing me with Misery's Woe

Her fire burns brightest after Midnight

When she haunted my feeble sanity

Cursing me into dust of desire

Unjust torment for my humanity

120

i despise this immortal life
waking up into this accursed land
a place where evil lives
to keep me locked in chains

evil brought into the world
through the mouths of dogs who are people
dogs who bite with sharpened teeth
people who bite with sharpened tongues

computers, technology
the salvation of man's flesh will be the death of him
his living body will become a dead carcass
drying in the sands of ages

times of the present
years far into unseen days and nights
birds will feast upon the diseased carrion man
which oversaw his own devastation

in hilarious irony the animals will feast
laughing at what feeds them abundantly
Who among the condemned
does not despise this immortal life—

waking up into this accursed world
where the beginning is Fear
the middle is Pain
and the end is corruption and Death?

121

*A*ll Hail!

The Queen of this new age, Ruler of this Great Land of Plenty

She is a creature of Miracles, a Magician—

A devil with slight of hand

The finest education, a masters degree, even the occasional Doctorate

But she is only an unpaid chef, a chauffeur, a chamber maid for room and board

Monumental cash reserves, bottomless pockets of dollars,

Unlimited charging credit, yet she has no income!

She cooks all the time, yet she cannot cook

She drives constantly, yet she cannot drive worth a dilly

Mistress of the House, yet her children obey nothing she commands!

Queen of the House, yet her king treats her like a slave!

Unwilling victim of this modern syndrome

Endless smiles, hiding the reserves of misery

Woman, Mother…

Wife.

Jonathan Lovejoy

All Hail!

The long haired brunette named Carlotta—

Amazed when she opens her mouth—

And the name Carla comes out on its own!

And then spring comes to her kingdom,

And her three children join the requisite soccer team

And in four months her brunette mane is at shoulders length

And in six months is cropped as short as it can be!

The next season is a gradual lightening to dirty blonde

Then further coloring until All her dark'ned strands are gone

Now she is a yellow lilly in the Field of Like

Sameness that spreads like a disease

A perverted orderliness—

A manufactured stability—

A giving way to security—

Excluding others from the unspoken elite

Happy pretty girls and boys and women

Angels of Grand Harwich Estates, Hobgoblins of Harwich

Smiling to mask the throat of doom

Laughing away the Ghost of Sorrow

Elizabethan

All Hail!

The Queen of this New Age

Our Lady of Likeness

Ruler in this Land of Plenty

Jonathan Lovejoy

22nd Assembly

122

White dragon flew the Land of Dreams

From my homeland to infinity

I searched far and wide the Wealthen Stream—

Grieving for the Land of Plenty

This dragon flew me high and low

In power of where I must command

I looked beyond the Azurean Glow

To the shores of a fair and distant land

But nowhere among the dragon's flight

Did I see my Golden Harvest Loom

So I rode upon the winds of might

Drifting to my house of doom

I grieved with hope from whence I came

From where the winged dragon flew

But I found my homeland just the same

The Land of Poverty I knew

123

Mercy falls as gentle rain
Winds breathe from the Throne of Grace
Gray skies weep for lives of men
Grieving, longing for a day of peace

From far across the Eastern Sea
The wind whirls into a behemoth
A white cloud of soothing rage
Swirling bands of Beautiful Death

Moving gracefully above the crashing sea
Thrashing waves of gentle fury
The Great Cloud traverses the watery plain
Whispering promises of devastation

Now the waters of the sounding sea
Arise in Power of Benevolence
Nature seeks refuge from her embrace
From this storm of her Malevolent Beauty

Mercy falls as gentle rain
Grieving for a day of peace

124

*W*isdom planted the Grove of Trees
Trees of sentimental youth
Leaves of every kind and color
Promising to grow

Every tree is a story grown
A harvest of the centuries
Knowledge surveys Arboreta's Row
Flourishing intrepidity

Elegance walks in humility
Among the Forest Grove of Trees
Wisdom planted these rows of life
A future in prosperity

Elizabethan

125

The name appears in the bars of music
Melodies blaze a Symphony of Light
The future sounds in the rhythm of life
Though indecision rules in strife

The Muse hath come in eerie spite
Tormenting this unrequited life
Harmonies expound a mighty insecurity
While visions confound the feeble sight

126

Rising above the Trees of Life
Despairs lift Autumn's fervent night
Burdens of pain in weary strife—
Drift beneath the Harvest Moon

Spirits of a tortured few
Elite in chosen misery
Beyond suffering unfruitful labour—
Rest beneath the Harvest Moon

Reprieve falls under cloak of night
Promises from the healing land
Mercy relieves grieving years—
Underneath the Harvest Moon

Elizabethan

127

From in the mists of high above
A woman fell to Earth below
As though she had nowhere to go
She drifted down to Earth

The woman fell from life above
Adrift with nowhere left to go
Drowned in waters of Hatteras
Found in waters of Evening Flow

As her children bereaved her soul in love
Her coffin lowered in the ground below
They grieved too great a grief to know
When their mother was laid to rest

They looked to a misty sky above
Knowing too great a pain to know
Wondering where it is they should go
As rain fell down to Earth

It rained in waters of Evening Flow
For the grieving down below

Jonathan Lovejoy

Elizabethan

23rd Assembly

128

From out of the golden Harvest Field
There arose a serpent to confound my reason
The snake crawled from the belly of a man
To live in this dark'ned season of plenty

Among those whose voice is soothed with kindness
Are some whose bowels are an accursed womb
A refuge for the black hearted serpentine
Waiting for his day of birth

In the lives of the naïve and the simple
There arises a serpent to confound their reason
A snake having crawled from the belly of a man
To contaminate the Harvest Season

129

*S*earched far and wide the Land of the Dead

Looking for a treasure of prosperity

To a stygian sky I looked for a sign

Finding nothing but blackness above me

As I walked to and fro in this Grieving Land

Looking for a measure of sincerity

From night infinity's darkest dread

A lost figure drifted aimlessly toward me

I braved the curious inclination for flight

To confront this figure with bravery

As I walked alone this eternal night

He moved towards me necromantically

I approached this creature in the Land of the Dead

Gazing in the face of humanity

Seeing only eyes devoid of life

Striking fear to the core of my sanity

I searched far and wide the Land of the Dead

Finding only a desert of inhumanity

130

A woman looked into the mirror
To see what there was to see
Locks of gray and white with silver
Where dark hair used to be

She bade farewell to youthful days
For all eternity—

But love still walked the winding road
Beneath the flowering tree
Her love did walk the winding road
In a place above the sea

In a land beyond the sea

131

*B*reezes kissed by winter's warning
Ghosts of what they once were
Children of nature's unkindness
Alive in their death season

Leaves…
Blowing over the grass
A wasteland of forgotten memories
Dancing in the autumn morning

Swirlings of brown and yellow—
Echoes of their life of green
Tossed in eternal sleep, on winds of uncaring cold
Seeking a new place to go

Somewhere, every leaf breathes with purpose—
Having direction—
Predestiny—
Appearing as chance to them who do not see

Jonathan Lovejoy

Who cannot see the leaves when they gather

Moving with thought—

Walking, running in fear

Talking with fervor, having anger

In groups, contemplating their course—

Deciding to go another way

Leaves…

Blowing over the grass, the wasteland

Devoid of the life that cannot see

Filled with the afterlife of green

Hiding, jumping into autumn breeze—

Flying to where they wish to be

24Th Assembly

Jonathan Lovejoy

132

*d*evastation—

  is planted in my brain

someday it will burst open

spilling poison into my mind

drowning my life force in

a haze of purple

until the haze turns black

around me

then my soul will leave

even before my eyes have ceased their vision

i wait fearfully, impatiently for the seed

to spill poison into my mind

killing this fragile body

i'm in

Elizabethan

133

*F*ound inside the House of White
A name appears in letters of life
Painted across the Innocence Wood
Images from a decade and four

Hatred revealed in pink and light
Scatter the disconnected floor
Bound by spiralings of metal
Enabled by the Chosen

Sustenence is poison death
Brought by pain's incarnate beauty
Echoes of promises unfulfilled
Resound across the Wilderness Plain

134

*H*igh above the Earth
these Three at sunset
glowing from the pink, orange hues
bands of power

hands of time above infinity
violet laced with echoes of crimson
these three underneath
backdrop of blue

across the Azurean Sea
beneath shores of cerulean
angelic eyes of power
these Three

protruding from nothingness
into this space
this time
one above in Creation

Elizabethan

one beneath in Redemption
one below in the Salvation of man
these Three
born from the hand of power

flung from marble skies of orange, pink
the blue of evening bands
these three draw back,
backward

moving into their mass of gray
moving backward
away from this Age of Mercy
power looms above the darkened shore

metallic tints of orange, gleaming,
when the points of final light have passed
dark lurks beneath the rim
in this final sunset

above the land of reason

These three, having moved away
Above this season of winter's eve
Eyes across glass infinity
When these three have gone

Jonathan Lovejoy

135

*U*nderneath gray skies
proven by the ocean waves
betrayal blows in upon arctic winds
raining snow upon the despised

gales whirl beneath the chemical path
above, around, sometimes below
rising it up beyond comprehension
cascading among the soaring waves

roaring paves the road to devastation
incredulous times of reason
seasons of plenty have vanished to oblivion
in Roman sensibilities

gnomes lurk beneath the surface of contempt
confounding times of drowning grief
above the hearkening voices of doom
corruption appears in a gigantic way

Elizabethan

among the arctic wind and waves
technology gives birth to the Admiral's Cave
a refugee from the madness wave
sadness holds the north region captive

underneath gray skies

Jonathan Lovejoy

136

Rain—

falling all around
Pain, a constant companion
having been told which way to go

Upon embarkment, storms of discontent
arising in this path
rising the swirling ocean
crashing the sounding sea

Having heard the truth laced with too many lies
directions unknown, courses unclear
history, unspoken
besmirches the only name given

Lies confound grieving souls
having been shown the truth
having been told which way to go
confronted by cruelty

Elizabethan

Eyes unfathomed
Unseeing, uncaring eyes
lusting for the blood of scribes—
unchosen

Fleet in the race to destruction
having been shown the truth
having been shown what is polar
the other side of sanity

Insane conglomerations of death
angels appear in foolish mocking—
how shall truth be found
when it is grown among the field of lies

laced with the poison of ages
clouds, gray and misery
despair forms in the words of thief—
stolen sadness

Appearing as a light to guide—
only to find the soul of emotion
bitterness, sorrow, misery, despair—
destruction, devastation and death

Jonathan Lovejoy

Accusations scream from the mouth of this storm

false accusations—

truth is confounded somewhere

having been told that truth is found

Fear of committal pours from weariness

afraid to believe lies, bound in shackles of beauty

carried away—

across the unrequited rain

25th Assembly

137

*H*never asked to be born
face of evil, lines of suffering
rivers of pain, a soul of dejection
born of an accursed woman

Nurtured by an uncaring father
thrust to a society with no feeling,
no center of morality
lines tell a story of pain

Destiny too deep to know
brows dark with knowledge of darkness
hair gray with wisdom of ages—
demonic lips curled

Scowling—
contempt beyond what is possible
eyes squinted with eternal defiance
expression replete with knowing, waiting

Elizabethan

Wondering what it was like for his victims to have died
wondering what it will feel like to die
needing pity, requiring understanding
understanding that none will be given

None has he given to a living soul
souls he sent to another world, an evil gift
abilities beyond comprehension
having not asked to be born

Asking not to be hated
wishing the tiniest whisper of compassion
knowing what it's like to kill
knowing what it feels like to die

Poison—
tasting blood of victims
feeling terror of death
born accursed

born to die

138

*T*here is a place beyond Tomorrow's World
A place of lost hopes and hidden dreams
Parallel to the Land of the Dead
Where souls live in ambiguity

Children roam the halls of squallor
Racked with disease and injury
Looking for reprieve from their life's pain
Having no knowedge of what they seek

Accepting trinkets with grateful smiles
Not believing they are worthless
Not knowing they are given with a stingy heart
Useless gifts bestowed without care

Without…

Underneath skies of apocalypse
Men and women play games
Laughing
Running to and fro

Elizabethan

From the Halls of Squallor
The priest emerges ineffectively
Laughing
Speaking of six days, six years, six hours more

Men of strength continue
Boasting of days that will never come
Women of strength continue
Confusing those who have lost their way

Some wander through Tomorrow's World
Seeking shelter from the violence
Finding nothing but inhospitable doors
Places barren with neglect...

And death

139

*F*rom the clouds…

Pours these colors of light

Colors of harvest hue

Light from the throne of grace

Given to this age of lost souls

Souls on the edge of cataclysm

Above sings a refrain of His restraint

Given in colors, power from clouds of mercy—

Even when light is diminished

And colors cannot be seen

Mercy hath fallen—

Upon the eyes of all who do not see

Colors of prophecy—

Light of promises fulfilled

Apocalyptic warnings—

Rumblings

Elizabethan

Shadings…

Telling of the end of this time

This age of thought

The disbelief of angels and men

140

When I see the Heart of Memory
I see you
Miss Mary...
You have come to me

My heart is weary
Exhausting this energy
I have tired of pushing
Pushing through the veil

From the other side of it rests nothing
Only another vast place of emptiness
Pointless voices of idiocy, lost
Screaming from beyond the veil

In the Heart of Memory
I hear you—
Miss Mary...
You have called to me

Elizabethan

Calling forth others who cannot care
Daylight shimmers with lying
False hope for despised and dispossessed
Still, even beyond grieving time

Mourning haunts the fervor of its calling
Mocking—
Taunting—
Calling for those who dare not hope

Speaking futures
Telling lies, riddles of truth
Telling truth in lying riddles
Confounding souls of reason

Showing fearful sights
Voices from darkness
Images of broken promises
Tearing hearts away from peace

When I see the Heart of Memory
I see you—
Miss Mary…
You have come to me

Insane graftings on wood of trees
Various lives in waiting
No mercy for them who wait for old decrees
Who have lost hope for a better time of living

141

*C*hildren of Light
There is no rest from pain
Two take hands in a wilderness alone
Both burning

Lost in desire for a time of life
Where there is no burning upon their skin
When there are no tears in crying eyes
Where there is no fear of dying

Where there is no place they need to go—
To escape the pain they are in

142

Flowers

Dying in this light of life

When sorrow grows in the field of like

resting

Burdens to carry down a weary path

where grief bestows

they are lonely travelers

upon this road of life

Jonathan Lovejoy

26th Assembly

Jonathan Lovejoy

143

*C*reatures, made of fur and color
Softness grows life and will
Playing like children upon a grassy plain
Bedecked in likenessess of men

In bewilderment unknown to passers by
All who look to them beware
As softness corrupts into crackling
Hardness breathes with demonic power

Bewitching morals to a death sleep
No understanding flows
In the minds of those who nurture the creatures
From the hearts of those who give them life

Who set them upon their game of grass
Pretty cherubs of comfort—
Black, lifeless eyes—
Smiling lips bearing fangs

Elizabethan

Deceiving, being deceived
Cloaked in a king's ransom of blue
Fawned by the aftermath of summer
In swirling storms of death and living

Jonathan Lovejoy

144

Resting above Evening Vale
The cloud brings life to she who rests
In the crimson land beyond Nightingale
Orange fades to violet, fading to the color of night

The cloud turns to blue
Changing itself into gray
Resting dark above Homeland Valley
Vanishing her sorrow away

Elizabethan

145

A man showed me above the city
Smiling promises of perpetuity
I followed him to his palace of goods
Hoping for this patronage to me

Drifting beneath skies of prosperity
Looking to the Horizon Tree
Obstacles loom in every path
Crushing me to poverty

I searched far throughout the city
Looking for the man of perpetuity
Finding his palace barren and void
Mocking patronage without duplicity

237

Jonathan Lovejoy

146

On our blue path among the stars
We circle an infinity
Pulled along by the Global Stream
Speeding towards our destiny

Lords and Kingpins, users and pushers
Families are torn apart
By the sea of thunder rising
By the greed of tears asunder

Drawn into Hordes of Legion
Entertained by the violent color
Waiting to kill…
Waiting to die

Somewhere in the midst of chaos
The seed of doubt remains
Corrupting goodness into bile
Causing idle hands to lust for power

238

Elizabethan

We must return to the darkened room
To reverse our path to dark eternity
A path leading to worlds unknown
Breaking into bands of animosity

We are told by the elite
That our path through the storm is done and complete
She will take no particular offence
When told the sign of the earthquake is wrong

On our blue path among the stars
We circle an infinity

Again and again
All roads lead to the barren plain
Around and around
Beneath the skies of eternity and grief

Rising into Calbot's Place
Having no energy for the present
But the Idyllic Path is stopped
Buried underneath brimstone and fire

Human life goes to Heaven—
Transformed by a miracle

Jonathan Lovejoy

27th Assembly

Jonathan Lovejoy

147

*T*he poets!

Roaming these Ivory Shores

Gazing across insanity's ocean

Rising above the madness plain

148

One born under a cloud
Adrift upon a sea of delusion
Looking to mourn the inevitable passing
Into a spirit of freedom

Delusions of grandeur
Visit a soul condemned
One who has seen the end of this life
Wishing to mourn the inevitable passing

Two look forward, seeing hope
Knowing that success is their own
Having pity, secret disgust
For the third who is in their midst

Moving backward
Drowned in loathing
Unable to see the traveling path
Leading to the Land of the Dead

Jonathan Lovejoy

149

On the trail of the innocent
I stop to look outside my window
Outside, the cloud turns to black…
Moving devastation to my door!

Through the walls of means
Blasts a Vesuvian tempest
Murder would be a blessing
Over the cloud's way of killing

Hiding from fevered wind
From the mighty wind of chaos
Until wrath blows no further warning
While I lay buried under debris…

I emerge from certain death
Into a world of darkened rain
Knowing the cloud has come to life
To bathe the world in Wisdom

Elizabethan

150

As the flower in Golden Flame

Their name is deadly to behold

At first beautiful

Then dreadful to look upon

151

There are points of realization
Moments that illuminate the senses
Until there is a perception
Of a greater force and power

The mind is then infused
With an irresistible assumption...
That life is perhaps nothing more
Than a series of predetermined events

The fulfillment...
Of a Divine plan and purpose
Destiny and Fate—
Through the will of God.

But for the accursed, for every living thing
There is shared a common gift
A focal point of strength
In the midst of prolonged suffering...

Elizabethan

It is the knowledge that time will pass—
And that all things must pass away

ABOUT THE AUTHOR

Jonathan Lovejoy is a graduate of the University of North Carolina at Greensboro, with a B.A. in Religious Studies. He currently lives in Winston Salem, North Carolina.

For more info on the author's life and career, visit jonathanlovejoy.com

www.ingramcontent.com/pod-product-compliance
Lightning Source LLC
Chambersburg PA
CBHW060232050426

42448CB00009B/1405